'My Heart's in the Highlands . . .'

AN ANTHOLOGY OF VERSE BY SCOTLAND'S BARD

Robert Burns

SELECTED BY

Elisabeth and Alexander Fraser

JARROLD COLOUR PUBLICATIONS

Norwich

INTRODUCTION

The great Scottish poet, Robert Burns, was born at Alloway, near Ayr, on 25 January 1759. His father, a small farmer or 'cotter', did his best to make sure that his son received a good education and for this purpose he employed a teacher, William Murdoch. Burns later wrote: 'I was a good deal noted for a retentive memory and a stubborn, sturdy "something" in my disposition. I made an excellent English scholar and by ten or eleven I was absolutely a critic in substantives, verbs and particles.' He also studied as many books of great verse as he could, including Shakespeare, Milton and Pope, and at the same time he absorbed the local folk-songs. He was thus well equipped to write in both formal English and the more vital Lowland Scots language, and was by no means the 'heaven-taught ploughboy' that he is sometimes supposed to have been.

For some years Burns worked on the family farm, ploughing and reaping, and he wrote his first poem at the age of fourteen for a girl who worked with him in the fields. After his father's death in 1784, Robert and his brother Gilbert leased the nearby Mossgiel Farm near Mauchline, and it was while working on this farm that Burns composed some of his best-known verses, such as *The Jolly Beggars*, *To a Mountain Daisy* and *To a Mouse*.

The farming enterprise proved a failure, however, and at about the same time his sweetheart, Jean Armour, was forbidden to see Burns by her father. Burns seriously considered emigration, and in order to raise the necessary money he published the Kilmarnock edition of his *Poems Chiefly in the Scottish Dialect* in 1786. They were an overnight success and Burns was encouraged to go to Edinburgh, where he published a second enlarged edition of the poems in 1787. With the proceeds (about £500 – a considerable sum of money in those days) he was able to undertake a grand tour of the Highlands, and on his return he bought a farm of his own at Ellisland, Dumfries.

Burns had had many love affairs in the past, most notably with the beautiful Mary Campbell, but now he seemed ready to settle down and in 1788 he married 'Bonnie Jean', Jean Armour, who had been the inspiration for many of his poems. The next year Burns was appointed an exciseman and he held this position until his death. In 1791 he moved to Dumfries and four years later joined the Dumfries Volunteers Corps. He died on 21 July 1796, at the early age of thirty-seven, of rheumatic fever caught in the pursuit of his duties as an exciseman, and he was buried with full military honours in St Michael's Churchyard, Dumfries.

Robert Burns lived at a time when the traditional Scottish mode of writing and speech was being overtaken by the more formalised English language and at first he succumbed to this. His poetry is undoubtedly at its best, however, when he turned away from formalisation and began to deal with the native Scottish themes, traditions and language. He was a great wit and a great satirist, but is probably most famous for the part he played in preserving the traditional Scottish songs, which he collected avidly and then remodelled. *Auld Lang Syne* is a prime example. Burns wrote of these songs: 'Those who think that composing a Scotch song is a trifling business, let them try.' His remodelling was not always an improvement, however, as he sentimentalised and consequently weakened some of the more direct and earthy of the ballads, but his best songs and poems are renowned for their humour, native vitality and intimacy of language. Although some critics have complained that the language is too local to be readily understandable, it is an important and, indeed, an intrinsic part of the life he describes so well.

MY HEART'S IN THE HIGHLANDS

The first half stanza of this song is old.

My heart's in the Highlands, my heart is not here;
My heart's in the Highlands, a-chasing the deer;
A-chasing the wild deer, and following the roe –
My heart's in the Highlands wherever I go.

Farewell to the Highlands, farewell to the North,
The birthplace of valour, the country of worth
Wherever I wander, wherever I rove,
The hills of the Highlands for ever I love.

Farewell to the mountains high cover'd with snow;
Farewell to the straths and green valleys below;
Farewell to the forests and wild-hanging woods;
Farewell to the torrents and loud-pouring floods.

My heart's in the Highlands, my heart is not here;
My heart's in the Highlands a-chasing the deer;
A-chasing the wild deer, and following the roe –
My heart's in the Highlands wherever I go.

WILLIE WASTLE'S WIFE

*Written in the old kitchen (now the Bar) of the
Crook Inn, Tweedsmuir.*

Willie Wastle dwalt on Tweed,
The spot they ca'd it Linkumdoddie;
Willie was a wabster gude,
Cou'd stown a clue wi' ony bodie;
He had a wife was dour and din,
O, Tinkler Maidgie was her mither:
Sic a wife as Willie had –
I wad na gie a button for her!

She has an e'e, she has but ane,
The cat has twa the very colour;
Five rusty teeth forbye a stump,
A clapper tongue wad deave a miller;
A whiskin beard about her mou,
Her nose and chin they threaten ither:
Sic a wife . . .

She's bow – hough'd, she's hem shin'd,
Ae limpin leg a hand-breed shorter;
She's twisted right, she's twisted left,
To balance fair in ilka quarter:
She has a lump upon her breast,
The twin o' that upon her shouther:
Sic a wife . . .

Auld baudrons by the ingle sits,
An' wi' her loof her face a washin;
But Willie's wife is nae sae trig:
She dights her grunzie wi' a hushion;
Her walie nieves like midden-creels,
Her face wad fyle the Logan Water:
Sic a wife . . .

Wabster – weaver
Forbye – besides
Mou – mouth
Bow-hough'd – bandy-legged
Ilka – every
Ingle – fireside
Trig – dainty
Fyle – pollute
Midden-creels – manure baskets

Dour and din – sulky, ill coloured
Deave – deafen
Ither – one another
Hand-breed – hand-breadth
Baudrons – cat
Loof – paw
Dights – wipes
Walie nieves – huge fists

EPIGRAM TO A SCRIMPIT NATURE

Written by the poet on a window pane at the Black Bull Inn, Moffat. The original pane of glass on which this poem was written is now in a museum in Moscow, Russia.

> Ask why God made the gem so small
> And why so huge the granite.
> Because God meant mankind should set
> The higher value on it!

I DREAM'D I LAY WHERE
FLOWERS WERE SPRINGING

Composed when the poet was seventeen.

I dream'd I lay where flowers were springing
  Gaily in the sunny beam,
Listening to the wild birds singing
  By a falling crystal stream:
Straight the sky grew black and daring;
  Through the woods the whirlwinds rave
Trees with agèd arms were warring,
  O'er the swelling, drumlie wave.

Such was my life's deceitful morning,
  Such the pleasures I enjoy'd;
But lang or noon, loud tempests storming
  A' my flowery bliss destroy'd.
Though fickle Fortune has deceived me,
  (She promised fair, and perform'd but ill,)
Of mony a joy and hope bereaved me,
  I bear a heart shall support me still.

Drumlie – muddy

LINES

Written in Friars' Carse Hermitage, on the banks of the
Nith. The first six lines were written with a diamond
on a window of the hermitage.

Thou whom chance may hither lead,
Be thou clad in russet weed,
Be thou deckt in silken stole,
Grave these maxims on thy soul:

Life is but a day at most,
Sprung from night, in darkness lost;
Day, how rapid in its flight –
Day, how few must see the night;
Hope not sunshine every hour,
Fear not clouds will always lower.
Happiness is but a name,
Make content and ease thy aim;
Ambition is a meteor gleam;
Fame an idle, restless dream:
Pleasures, insects on the wing
Round Peace, the tenderest flower of Spring!

Those that sip the dew alone,
Make the butterflies thy own;
Those that would the bloom devour,
Crush the locusts – save the flower.
For the future be prepared,
Guard whatever thou canst guard:
But, thy utmost duly done,
Welcome what thou canst not shun.
Follies past give thou to air,
Make their consequence thy care:

Keep the name of man in mind,
And dishonour not thy kind.
Reverence with lowly heart
Him whose wondrous work thou art;
Keep His goodness still in view,
Thy trust – and thy example, too.

Stranger, go! Heaven be thy guide!
Quoth the Beadsman on Nithside.

ADDRESS TO THE TOOTHACHE

*Written when the author was grievously tormented by
that disorder.*

My curse upon thy venom'd stang,
That shoots my tortured gums alang;
And through my lugs gies mony a twang,
        Wi' gnawing vengeance;
Tearing my nerves wi' bitter pang,
        Like racking engines!

When fevers burn, or ague freezes,
Rheumatics gnaw, or cholic squeezes;
Our neighbour's sympathy may ease us,
        Wi' pitying moan;
But thee – thou hell o' a' diseases,
        Aye mocks our groan!

Adown my beard the slavers trickle!
I kick the wee stools o'er the mickle,
As round the fire the giglets keckle,
        To see me loup;
While, raving mad, I wish a heckle
        Were in their doup.

Of a' the numerous human dools,
Ill hairsts, daft bargains, cutty-stools,
Or worthy friends raked i' the mools,
        Sad sight to see!
The tricks o' knaves, or fash o' fools,
        Thou bear'st the gree.

Where'er that place be priests ca' hell,
Whence a' the tones o' misery yell,
And rankèd plagues their numbers tell,
    In dreadfu' raw,
Thou, Toothache, surely bear'st the bell
    Amang them a'!

O thou grim mischief-making chiel,
That gars the notes of discord squeel,
Till daft mankind aft dance a reel
    In gore a shoe thick,
Gie a' the faes o' Scotland's weal
    A towmond's toothache!

Lugs – ears   Giglets – children   Keckle – laugh
Loup – jump   Heckle – flax comb   Doup – breech
Dools – sorrows   Hairsts – harvests
Cutty-stools – stools of repentance   Mools – graves
Fash – trouble   Gree – superiority   Raw – row
Gars – makes   Faes – foes   Weal – welfare
Towmond – Twelve months

THE SELKIRK GRACE

*An impromptu verse on being asked to say grace
at dinner while visiting the Earl of Selkirk.*

Some hae meat, and canna eat,
    And some wad eat that want it;
But we hae meat, and we can eat,
    And sae the Lord be thankit.

THE YOUNG HIGHLAND ROVER

Loud blaw the frosty breezes,
  The snaws the mountains cover;
Like winter on me seizes,
  Since my young Highland rover
  Far wanders nations over.
Where'er he go, where'er he stray,
  May Heaven be his warden;
Return him safe to fair Strathspey,
  And bonny Castle-Gordon!

The trees, now naked groaning,
  Shall soon wi' leaves be hinging,
The birdies, dowie moaning,
  Shall a' be blithely singing,
  And every flower be springing.
Sae I'll rejoice the lee-lang day,
  When by his mighty warden
My youth's return'd to fair Strathspey,
  And bonny Castle-Gordon.

Dowie – sadly   Lee-lang – life-long

OUT OVER THE FORTH

Out over the Forth I look to the north,
  But what is the north and its Highlands to me?
The south nor the east gie ease to my breast,
  The far foreign land, or the wild-rolling sea.

But I look to the west, when I gae to rest,
  That happy my dreams and my slumbers may be;
For far in the west lives he I lo'e best,
  The lad that is dear to my baby and me.

POLLY STEWART

*Written on a window pane at the Globe Inn, Dumfries, which
Burns frequently visited and where his chair can still be seen.
Polly Stewart was the daughter of the factor on the Closeburn
estate, and a close friend of Burns.*

O lovely Polly Stewart,
O Charming Polly Stewart,
There's not a flower that blooms in May
That's half so fair as thou art.

ROBIN

When the poet's father was riding to fetch a doctor to assist at Robert's birth, he helped an old gipsy woman to cross a flooded stream. In gratitude she visited the new-born child and made the predictions incorporated in this song.

There was a lad was born in Kyle,
But whatna day o' whatna style,
I doubt it's hardly worth the while
 To be sae nice wi' Robin.
  Robin was a rovin' boy,
   Rantin' rovin', rantin' rovin';
  Robin was a rovin' boy,
   Rantin' rovin' Robin!

Our monarch's hindmost year but ane
Was five and twenty days begun,
'Twas then a blast o' Januar win'
 Blew hansel in on Robin.

The gossip keekit in his loof,
Quo' she, wha lives will see the proof,
This waly boy will be nae coof –
 I think we'll ca' him Robin.

He'll hae misfortunes great and sma',
But aye a heart aboon them a';
He'll be a credit till us a',
 We'll a' be proud o' Robin.

But, sure as three times three mak nine,
I see, by ilka score and line,
This chap will dearly like our kin',
   So leeze me on thee, Robin.

Guid faith, quo' she, I doubt ye'se gar
The bonny lasses lie aspar,
But twenty fauts ye may hae waur,
   So blessin's on thee, Robin!

Rantin' – merry   Hansel – birth gift   Gossip – old woman
Keekit – looked   Loof – palm
Waly – fine   Coof – fool   Ilka – every
Leeze – a term of endearment   Gar – make   Aspar – astride

TO A LOUSE

On seeing one on a lady's bonnet at church.

Ha! whare ye gaun, ye crowlin' ferlie!
Your impudence protects you sairly:
I canna say but ye strunt rarely,
  Owre gauze and lace;
Though, faith, I fear ye dine but sparely
  On sic a place.

Ye ugly, creepin', blastit wonner,
Detested, shunn'd, by saunt and sinner,
How dare ye set your fit upon her,
  Sae fine a lady?
Gae somewhere else, and seek your dinner
  On some poor body.

Swith, in some beggar's haffet squattle;
There ye may creep, and sprawl, and sprattle
Wi' ither kindred, jumping cattle,
  In shoals and nations;
Whare horn nor bane ne'er daur unsettle
  Your thick plantations.

Now haud you there, ye're out o' sight,
Below the fatt'rils, snug and tight;
Na, faith ye yet! ye'll no be right
  Till ye've got on it,
The very tapmost, towering height
  O' Miss's bonnet.

My sooth! right bauld ye set your nose out,
As plump and gray as ony grozet:
Oh for some rank, mercurial rozet,
    Or fell, red smeddum,
I'd gie ye sic a hearty doze o't,
    Wad dress your droddum!

I wadna been surprised to spy
You on an auld wife's flannen toy:
Or aiblins some bit duddie boy,
    On's wyliecoat:
But Miss's fine Lunardi! fie!
    How daur ye do't?

O Jenny, dinna toss your head,
And set your beauties a' abread!
Ye little ken what cursèd speed
    The blastie's makin'!
Thae winks and finger-ends, I dread,
    Are notice takin'!

Oh wad some power the giftie gie us
To see oursels as others see us!
It wad frae mony a blunder free us,
    And foolish notion:
What airs in dress and gait wad lea'e us,
    And even devotion!

Crowlin' ferlie – crawling wonder   Strunt – strut
Fit – foot   Swith – quick   Haffet – hair   Squattle – crawl
Sprattle – scramble   Horn, bane – comb
Fatt'rils – ribbon ends   Grozet – gooseberry   Rozet – rosin
Smeddum – powder   Droddum – breech
Flannen toy – flannel cap   Aiblins – perhaps
Duddie – ragged   Wyliecoat – flannel waistcoat
Lunardi – fashionable type of bonnet   Abread – all about
Blastie – dwarf   Thae – those   Gait – manner

SONNET

*On hearing a thrush sing in a morning walk; written
25 January 1793, the birthday of the author.*

Sing on, sweet thrush, upon the leafless bough,
   Sing on, sweet bird, I listen to thy strain:
   See, agèd Winter, 'mid his surly reign,
At thy blithe carol clears his furrow'd brow.

So in lone Poverty's dominion drear,
   Sits meek Content with light unanxious heart,
   Welcomes the rapid moments, bids them part,
Nor asks if they bring aught to hope or fear.

I thank Thee, Author of this opening day!
   Thou whose bright sun now gilds yon orient skies!
   Riches denied, Thy boon was purer joys,
What wealth could never give nor take away!

Yet come, thou child of Poverty and Care;
The mite high Heaven bestow'd, that mite with thee I'll share.

THE BATTLE OF KILLIECRANKIE

*This song celebrates the battle where Viscount Dundee
fell in the moment of victory. The chorus is old.*

> Whare hae ye been sae braw, lad?
>   Whare hae ye been sae brankie, O?
> Oh, whare hae ye been sae braw, lad?
>   Cam ye by Killiecrankie, O?
> An ye had been whare I hae been,
>   Ye wadna been sae cantie, O;
> An ye had seen what I hae seen,
> On the braes o' Killiecrankie, O.
>
> I fought at land, I fought at sea;
>   At hame I fought my auntie, O;
> But I met the devil and Dundee,
>   On the braes o' Killiecrankie, O.
> The bauld Pitcur fell in a fur,
>   And Clavers got a clankie, O;
> Or I had fed an Athole gled,
> On the braes o' Killiecrankie, O.

Braw – handsome   Brankie – finely dressed
Cantie – merry   Braes – hills   Fur – furrow   Gled – kite

LINES

*Written with a pencil over the chimneypiece in the
parlour of the inn at Kenmore, Taymouth.*

Admiring Nature in her wildest grace,
These northern scenes with weary feet I trace;
O'er many a winding dale and painful steep,
The abodes of covey'd grouse and timid sheep,
My savage journey, curious, I pursue,
Till famed Breadalbane opens to my view, –
The meeting cliffs each deep-sunk glen divides,
The woods, wild scatter'd, clothe their ample sides;
The outstretching lake, embosom'd 'mong the hills,
The eye with wonder and amazement fills:
The Tay, meandering sweet in infant pride,
The palace, rising on its verdant side;
The lawns, wood-fringed in Nature's native taste;
The hillocks, dropt in Nature's careless haste;
The arches, striding o'er the new-born stream;
The village, glittering in the noontide beam –

Poetic ardours in my bosom swell,
Lone wandering by the hermit's mossy cell:
The sweeping theatre of hanging woods!
The incessant roar of headlong tumbling floods.

Here Poesy might wake her Heaven-taught lyre,
And look through Nature with creative fire;
Here, to the wrongs of Fate half-reconciled,
Misfortune's lighten'd steps might wander wild;
And Disappointment, in these lonely bounds,
Find balm to soothe her bitter, rankling wounds;
Here heart-struck Grief might heavenward stretch her scan,
And injured Worth forget and pardon man.

THE HIGHLAND LASSIE

*The heroine of this song was Mary Campbell, 'Highland Mary',
whom Burns might have married had it not been for her untimely
death in 1786.*

Nae gentle dames, though e'er sae fair,
Shall ever be my Muse's care:
Their titles a' are empty show;
Gie me my Highland Lassie, O.

Within the glen sae bushy, O,
Aboon the plains sae rushy, O,
I set me down wi' right good will,
To sing my Highland Lassie, O.

Oh, were yon hills and valleys mine,
Yon palace and yon gardens fine!
The world then the love should know
I bear my Highland Lassie, O.

But fickle Fortune frowns on me,
And I maun cross the raging sea!
But while my crimson currents flow,
I'll love my Highland Lassie, O.

Although through foreign climes I range,
I know her heart will never change,
For her bosom burns with honour's glow,
My faithful Highland Lassie, O.

For her I'll dare the billows' roar,
For her I'll trace the distant shore,
That Indian wealth may lustre throw
Around my Highland Lassie, O.

She has my heart, she has my hand,
By sacred truth and honour's band!
'Till the mortal stroke shall lay me low,
I'm thine, my Highland Lassie, O.

Fareweel the glen sae bushy, O!
Fareweel the plain sae rushy, O!
To other lands I now must go,
To sing my Highland Lassie, O!

Gentle – high-blooded

TO A MOUNTAIN DAISY

On turning one down with a plough in April 1786.

> Wee, modest, crimson-tippèd flower,
> Thou's met me in an evil hour;
> For I maun crush amang the stoure
>   Thy slender stem:
> To spare thee now is past my power,
>   Thou bonny gem.
>
> Alas! it's no thy neibor sweet,
> The bonny lark, companion meet,
> Bending thee 'mang the dewy weet,
>   Wi' speckled breast,
> When upward springing, blithe, to greet
>   The purpling east.
>
> Cauld blew the bitter-biting north
> Upon thy early, humble, birth;
> Yet cheerfully thou glinted forth
>   Amid the storm,
> Scarce rear'd above the parent earth
>   Thy tender form.
>
> The flaunting flowers our gardens yield,
> High sheltering woods and wa's maun shield;
> But thou, beneath the random bield
>   O' clod or stane,
> Adorns the histie stibble-field,
>   Unseen, alane.

There, in thy scanty mantle clad,
Thy snawie bosom sun-ward spread,
Thou lifts thy unassuming head
          In humble guise;
But now the share uptears thy bed,
          And low thou lies!

Such is the fate of artless maid,
Sweet floweret of the rural shade!
By love's simplicity betray'd,
          And guileless trust,
Till she, like thee, all soil'd, is laid
          Low i' the dust.

Such is the fate of simple bard,
On life's rough ocean luckless starr'd!
Unskilful he to note the card
          Of prudent lore,
Till billows rage, and gales blow hard,
          And whelm him o'er!

Such fate to suffering worth is given,
Who long with wants and woes has striven,
By human pride or cunning driven
          To misery's brink,
Till, wrench'd of every stay but Heaven,
          He, ruin'd, sink!

Even thou who mourn'st the Daisy's fate,
That fate is thine – no distant date;
Stern Ruin's ploughshare drives, elate,
          Full on thy bloom,
Till, crush'd beneath the furrow's weight,
          Shall be thy doom!

Stoure – dust   Glinted – peeped   Wa' – wall
Bield – shelter   Histie – barren

A RED, RED ROSE

An improvement of a street ballad.

Oh, my luve's like a red, red rose,
　That's newly sprung in June:
Oh, my luve's like the melodie
　That's sweetly play'd in tune.

As fair art thou, my bonny lass,
　So deep in luve am I;
And I will luve thee still, my dear,
　Till a' the seas gang dry.

Till a' the seas gang dry, my dear,
　And the rocks melt wi' the sun:
I will luve thee still, my dear,
　While the sands o' life shall run.

And fare thee weel, my only luve!
　And fare thee weel a while!
And I will come again, my luve,
　Though it were ten thousand mile.

COMING THROUGH THE RYE

Coming through the rye, poor body,
  Coming through the rye,
She draiglet a' her petticoatie,
  Coming through the rye.

O Jenny's a' wat, poor body,
  Jenny's seldom dry;
She draiglet a' her petticoatie,
  Coming through the rye.

Gin a body meet a body
  Coming through the rye;
Gin a body kiss a body –
  Need a body cry?

Gin a body meet a body
  Coming through the glen;
Gin a body kiss a body –
  Need the warld ken?

*Burns wrote this varied rendering of one of the verses with a
diamond on a window pane, which can still be seen, at the Globe
Inn, Dumfries.*

Gin a body meet a body
  Coming through the grain
Gin a body kiss a body
  The thing's a body's ain.

Draiglet – soiled Gin – if

TO A HAGGIS

*The haggis, a very palatable Scottish dish, is made
from minced offal of mutton, meal, suet and seasoning,
and boiled in a sheep's stomach.*

Fair fa' your honest, sonsie face,
Great chieftain o' the puddin' race!
Aboon them a' ye tak your place,
     Painch, tripe, or thairm:
Weel are ye worthy of a grace
     As lang's my arm.

The groaning trencher there ye fill,
Your hurdies like a distant hill,
Your pin wad help to mend a mill
     In time o' need,
While through your pores the dews distil
     Like amber bead.

His knife see rustic labour dight,
And cut you up wi' ready slight,
Trenching your gushing entrails bright
     Like ony ditch;
And then, oh, what a glorious sight,
     Warm-reekin', rich!

Then horn for horn they stretch and strive,
Deil tak the hindmost, on they drive,
Till all their weel-swall'd kytes belyve
     Are bent like drums;
Then auld guidman, maist like to rive,
     Bethankit hums.

Is there that owre his French ragoût,
Or olio that wad staw a sow,
Or fricassee wad mak her spew
    Wi' perfect scunner,
Looks down wi' sneering, scornfu' view
    On sic a dinner?

Poor devil! see him owre his trash,
As feckless as a wither'd rash,
His spindle-shank a guid whip-lash,
    His nieve a nit:
Through bloody flood or field to dash,
    Oh, how unfit!

But mark the rustic, haggis-fed,
The trembling earth resounds his tread,
Clap in his walie nieve a blade,
     He'll mak it whissle;
And legs, and arms, and heads will sned,
     Like taps o' thrissle.

Ye powers wha mak mankind your care,
And dish them out their bill o' fare,
Auld Scotland wants nae skinking ware
     That jaups in luggies;
But if ye wish her gratefu' prayer,
     Gie her a haggis!

Fair fa' – good luck to   Sonsie – comely   Painch – belly
Thairm – small intestine   Hurdies – hips   Dight – seize
Warm-reekin' – smoking   Weel-swall' – well swollen
Kyte – belly   Belyve – at once   Rive – burst
Bethankit – say grace   Staw – satiate   Scunner – loathing
Feckless – pithless   Rash – rush   Nieve – fist
Nit – nut   Walie – goodly   Sned – cut off
Skinking – watery   Ware – thin stuff   Jaups – splashes
Luggies – wooden bowls

BONNY DUNDEE

Second verse

My blessin's upon thy sweet wee lippie,
  My blessin's upon thy bonny eebree!
Thy smiles are sae like my blithe sodger laddie,
  Thou's aye be dearer and dearer to me!
But I'll big a bower on yon bonny banks,
  Where Tay rins wimplin' by sae clear;
And I'll cleed thee in the tartan sae fine,
  And mak thee a man like thy daddie dear.

Eebree – eyebrow   Sodger – soldier   Big – build
Wimplin' – meandering

HERE STUARTS ONCE . . .

Written by Burns in 1787, on the glass of a window in one of the bedrooms, now called the 'Burns Suite', at the Golden Lion Hotel, Stirling. (The actual sheet of glass is no longer in the hotel.)

> Here Stuarts once in glory reigned,
> And laws for Scotland's weal ordain'd;
> But now unroofed their palace stands
> Their Sceptre's sway'd by other hands;
> The injured Stuart line is gone,
> A Race outlandish fills their throne,
> An idiot race to honour lost,
> Who know them best, despise them most.

On being told that the above verse would affect his prospects, the poet took his diamond pin and wrote the following additional lines on the glass:

> Rash mortal and slanderous poet,
>   thy name
> Shall no longer appear in the records
>   of fame:
> Dost not know that old Mansfield,
>   Who writes like the Bible,
> Says, 'the more 'tis a truth sir,
>   The more 'tis a libel'.

BRUCE'S ADDRESS TO HIS
ARMY AT BANNOCKBURN

*This song was written to fit an air supposed to be
Robert Bruce's march at the Battle of Bannockburn.*

Scots, wha hae wi' Wallace bled,
Scots, wham Bruce has aften led;
Welcome to your gory bed,
  Or to Victory!

Now's the day, and now's the hour;
See the front o' battle lour;
See approach proud Edward's power –
  Chains and slavery!

Wha will be a traitor knave?
Wha can fill a coward's grave?
Wha sae base as be a slave?
  Let him turn and flee!

Wha, for Scotland's king and law,
Freedom's sword will strongly draw;
Freeman stand, or freeman fa',
  Let him follow me!

By Oppression's woes and pains!
By your sons in servile chains!
We will drain our dearest veins,
  But they shall be free!

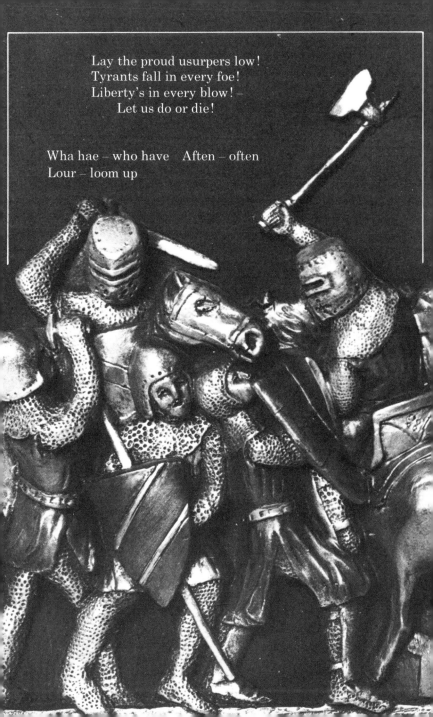

Lay the proud usurpers low!
Tyrants fall in every foe!
Liberty's in every blow! –
Let us do or die!

Wha hae – who have   Aften – often
Lour – loom up

TO A MOUSE

On turning up her nest with the plough, November 1785.

Wee, sleekit, cowrin', tim'rous beastie,
Oh, what a panic's in thy breastie!
Thou needna start awa' sae hasty,
    Wi' bickering brattle!
I wad be laith to rin and chase thee,
    Wi' murd'ring pattle!

I'm truly sorry man's dominion
Has broken nature's social union,
And justifies that ill opinion
      Which maks thee startle
At me, thy poor earth-born companion,
      And fellow-mortal!

I doubt na, whyles, but thou may thieve;
What then? poor beastie, thou maun live!
A daimen icker in a thrave
      'S a sma' request:
I'll get a blessin' wi' the lave,
      And never miss't!

Thy wee bit housie, too, in ruin!
Its silly wa's the win's are strewin'!
And naething now to big a new ane
      O' foggage green!
And bleak December's winds ensuin',
      Baith snell and keen!

Thou saw the fields laid bare and waste,
And weary winter comin' fast,
And cozie here, beneath the blast,
      Thou thought to dwell,
Till, crash! the cruel coulter past
      Out through thy cell.

That wee bit heap o' leaves and stibble
Has cost thee mony a weary nibble!
Now thou's turn'd out for a' thy trouble,
      But house or hauld,
To thole the winter's sleety dribble,
      And cranreuch cauld!

But, Mousie, thou art no thy lane,
In proving foresight may be vain:
The best-laid schemes o' mice and men
        Gang aft a-gley,
And lea'e us nought but grief and pain
        For promised joy.

Still thou art blest, compared wi' me!
The present only toucheth thee:
But, och! I backward cast my ee
        On prospects drear!
And forward, though I canna see,
        I guess and fear.

Sleekit – shy, smooth-haired   Cowrin' – cowering
Bickering – scurrying   Brattle – hurry, run
Pattle – plough spade   Whyles – sometimes
Daimen icker – ear of corn   Thrave – 24 sheaves of corn
Lave – remainder   Wa's – walls   Big – build
Foggage – foliage   Snell – sharp   Cozie – comfortable
Coulter – plough-share blade   But – without
Hauld – refuge   Thole – endure – Cranreuch – hoar frost
No thy lane – not alone   Gang aft a-gley – go often awry

THE RANTIN' DOG THE DADDIE O'T

Written for Elizabeth Paton, a servant in
Burns's mother's house.

> Oh wha my babie-clouts will buy?
> Oh wha will tent me when I cry?
> Wha will kiss me where I lie? –
>   The rantin' dog the daddie o't.
>
> Oh wha will own he did the faut?
> Oh wha will buy the groanin' maut?
> Oh wha will tell me how to ca't? –
>   The rantin' dog the daddie o't.
>
> When I mount the creepie-chair,
> Wha will sit beside me there?
> Gie me Rob, I'll seek nae mair,
>   The rantin' dog the daddie o't.
>
> Wha will crack to me my lane?
> Wha will mak me fidgin-fain?
> Wha will kiss me o'er again? –
>   The rantin' dog the daddie o't.

Rantin' – making merry   Babie-clouts – baby clothes
Tent – heed   Maut – ale to drink to child's birth
Creepie-chair – stool of repentance   Crack – talk
Lane – self   Fidgin-fain – fidget with delight

AULD LANG SYNE

Should auld acquaintance be forgot,
  And never brought to min'?
Should auld acquaintance be forgot,
  And days o' lang syne?

  For auld lang syne, my dear,
    For auld lang syne,
    We'll tak a cup o' kindness yet
      For auld lang syne!

We twa hae run about the braes,
  And pu'd the gowans fine;
But we've wander'd mony a weary foot
  Sin' auld lang syne.

We twa hae paidl't i' the burn,
  Frae morning sun till dine:
But seas between us braid hae roar'd
  Sin' auld lang syne.

And here's a hand, my trusty fiere,
  And gies a hand o' thine;
And we'll tak a cup o' kindness yet,
  For auld lang syne!

And surely ye'll be your pint-stoup,
  And surely I'll be mine;
And we'll tak a cup o' kindness yet,
  For auld lang syne.

Auld lang syne – former days and friends   Braes – hills
Gowans – daisies   Braid – broad   Fiere – friend
Willie-waught – friendly draught   Pint-stoup – tankard

10. Fragment ——— Auld lang syne ———

And surely ye'll be your pint stoup,
    And surely I'll be mine;
And we'll tak a cup o' kindness yet,
    For auld lang syne. —

We twa hae run about the braes,
    And pou't the gowans fine;
But we've wandered mony a weary
    Sin auld lang syne.

We twa hae paidl't in the burn
    O frae morning sun till dine
But seas between us braid hae roar
    Sin auld lang syne. —

And there's a hand,
    And gies a hand
nd we'll tak a right
    For auld lang

WOMEN'S MINDS

Though women's minds, like winter winds,
   May shift and turn, and a' that,
The noblest breast adores them maist,
   A consequence I draw that.

   For a' that, and a' that,
     And twice as muckle's a' that,
   The bonny lass that I lo'e best
     She'll be my ain for a' that.

Great love I bear to all the fair,
   Their humble slave, and a' that;
But lordly will, I hold it still,
   A mortal sin to thraw that.

But there is ane aboon the lave,
   Has wit, and sense, and a' that;
A bonny lass, I like her best,
   And wha a crime dare ca' that?

Muckle – much   Thraw – frustrate   Lave – rest

CASSILLIS' BANKS

Now bank and brae are claithed in green,
　And scatter'd cowslips sweetly spring;
By Girvan's fairy-haunted stream
　The birdies flit on wanton wing.
To Cassillis' banks, when e'ening fa's,
　There, wi' my Mary, let me flee,
There catch her ilka glance of love,
　The bonny blink o' Mary's ee!

The chield wha boasts o' warld's walth
　Is aften laird o' meikle care;
But Mary, she is a' mine ain –
　Ah! fortune canna gie me mair!
Then let me range by Cassillis' banks,
　Wi' her, the lassie dear to me,
And catch her ilka glance o' love,
　The bonny blink o' Mary's ee!

Brae – hill　Ilka – every　Meikle – much

ON SCARING SOME WATER-FOWL IN LOCH TURIT

A wild scene among the hills of Ochtertyre

Why, ye tenants of the lake,
For me your watery haunts forsake?
Tell me, fellow-creatures, why
At my presence thus you fly?
Why disturb your social joys,
Parent, filial, kindred ties? –
Common friend to you and me,

Nature's gifts to all are free:
Peaceful keep your dimpling wave,
Busy feed, or wanton lave;
Or, beneath the sheltering rock,
Bide the surging billow's shock.

Conscious, blushing for our race,
Soon, too soon, your fears I trace.
Man, your proud usurping foe,
Would be lord of all below:
Plumes himself in freedom's pride,
Tyrant stern to all beside.
The eagle, from the cliffy brow,
Marking you his prey below,
In his breast no pity dwells,
Strong necessity compels:
But man, to whom alone is given
A ray direct from pitying Heaven,
Glories in his heart humane –
And creatures for his pleasure slain.
In these savage, liquid plains,
Only known to wandering swains,
Where the mossy rivulet strays,
Far from human haunts and ways;
All on nature you depend,
And life's poor season peaceful spend.
Or, if man's superior might
Dare invade your native right,
On the lofty ether borne,
Man with all his powers you scorn:
Swiftly seek, on clanging wings,
Other lakes and other springs;
And the foe you cannot brave
Scorn at least to be his slave.

THE PIPER

A Fragment

There came a piper out o' Fife,
  I watna what they ca'd him;
He play'd our cousin Kate a spring
  When fient a body bade him;
And aye the mair he hotch'd and blew,
  The mair that she forbade him.

Spring – lively tune   Fient a – the devil a
Hotch'd – jerked about

A FRAGMENT

One night as I did wander,
  When corn begins to shoot,
I sat me down to ponder
  Upon an auld tree root:
Auld Ayr ran by before me,
  And bicker'd to the seas;
A cushat croodled o'er me,
That echo'd through the braes.

Bicker'd – raced   Cushat – wood pigeon
Croodled – cooed   Braes – hills

THE BIRKS OF ABERFELDY

Composed after visiting the falls of Moness near Aberfeldy.

Bonny lassie, will ye go,
Will ye go, will ye go;
Bonny lassie, will ye go
   To the birks of Aberfeldy?

Now simmer blinks on flowery braes,
And o'er the crystal streamlet plays;
Come, let us spend the lightsome days
   In the birks of Aberfeldy.

While o'er their heads the hazels hing,
The little birdies blithely sing,
Or lightly flit on wanton wing
   In the birks of Aberfeldy.

The braes ascend, like lofty wa's,
The foaming stream deep-roaring fa's,
O'erhung wi' fragrant spreading shaws,
   The birks of Aberfeldy.

The hoary cliffs are crown'd wi' flowers,
White o'er the linns the burnie pours,
And rising, weets wi' misty showers
   The birks of Aberfeldy.

Let Fortune's gifts at random flee,
They ne'er shall draw a wish frae me,
Supremely blest wi' love and thee,
   In the birks of Aberfeldy.

Birks – birches   Braes – hills   Wa's – walls
Shaws – woods   Linns – waterfalls

MY LOVE SHE'S BUT A LASSIE YET

My love she's but a lassie yet,
  My love she's but a lassie yet;
We'll let her stand a year or twa,
  She'll no be half sae saucy yet.
I rue the day I sought her, O,
  I rue the day I sought her, O;
Wha gets her needna say she's woo'd,
  But he may say he's bought her, O!

Come, draw a drap o' the best o't yet;
  Come, draw a drap o' the best o't yet;
Gae seek for pleasure where ye will,
  But here I never miss'd it yet.
We're a' dry wi' drinking o't;
  We're a' dry wi' drinking o't;
The minister kiss'd the fiddler's wife,
  And couldna preach for thinkin' o't.

A BARD'S EPITAPH

Written by Burns for himself.

Is there a whim-inspirèd fool,
Owre fast for thought, owre hot for rule,
Owre blate to seek, owre proud to snool?
    Let him draw near;
And owre this grassy heap sing dool,
      And drap a tear.

Is there a bard of rustic song,
Who, noteless, steals the crowds among,
That weekly this area throng?
    Oh, pass not by!
But, with a frater-feeling strong,
      Here heave a sigh.

Is there a man, whose judgment clear
Can others teach the course to steer,
Yet runs himself life's mad career
    Wild as the wave?
Here pause – and, through the starting tear,
      Survey this grave.

The poor inhabitant below
Was quick to learn, and wise to know,
And keenly felt the friendly glow,
    And softer flame;
But thoughtless follies laid him low,
      And stain'd his name!

Reader, attend – whether thy soul
Soars fancy's flights beyond the pole,
Or darkling grubs this earthly hole,
        In low pursuit;
Know, prudent, cautious self-control
        Is wisdom's root.

Owre – over   Blate – bashful   Snool – be obsequious
Dool – sorrowfully